FOR ORGANS, PIANOS & ELECTRONIC KEYBOARDS

E-Z PLAY® TODAY

183

WEST SIDE STORY®

Based on a conception of Jerome Robbins

Book by

Arthur Laurents

Music by

Leonard Bernstein®

Lyrics by

Stephen Sondheim

Entire original production
directed and choreographed by
Jerome Robbins

T0081848

CONTENTS

ISBN 978-1-4234-3734-5

LEONARD
BERNSTEIN
Music Publishing
Company LLC

BOOSEY & HAWKES

HAL•LEONARD®
CORPORATION

7777 W. BLUEMOUND RD. P.O. BOX 13819 MILWAUKEE, WI 53213

Visit Hal Leonard Online at
www.halleonard.com

America

Registration 8
Rhythm: 6/8 March

Lyrics by Stephen Sondheim
Music by Leonard Bernstein

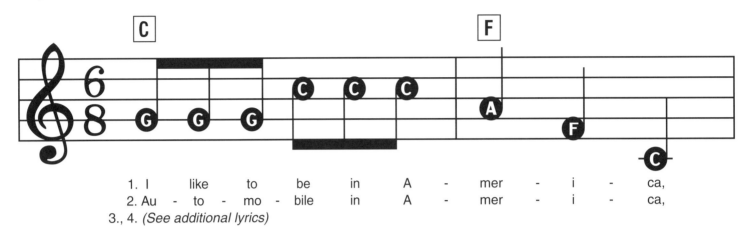

1. I like to be in A - mer - i - ca,
2. Au - to - mo - bile in A - mer - i - ca,
3., 4. *(See additional lyrics)*

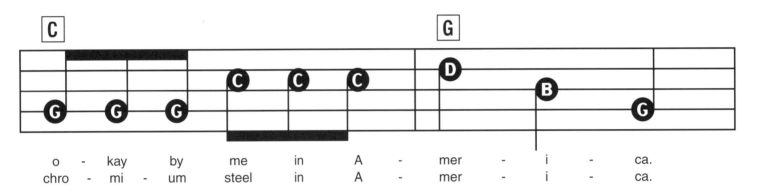

o - kay by me in A - mer - i - ca.
chro - mi - um steel in A - mer - i - ca.

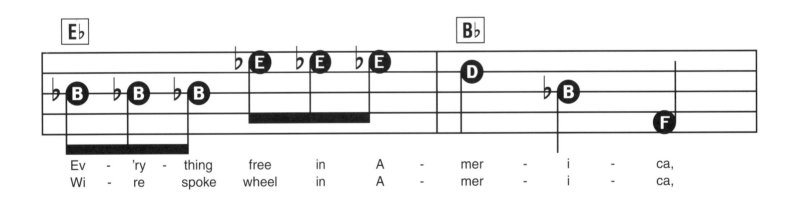

Ev - 'ry - thing free in A - mer - i - ca,
Wi - re spoke wheel in A - mer - i - ca,

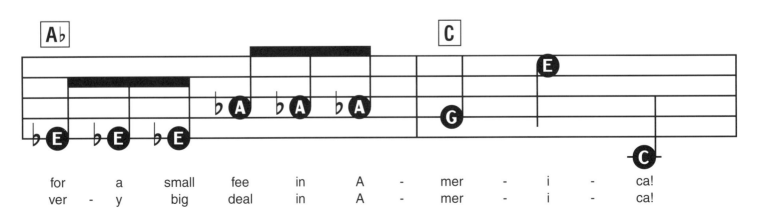

for a small fee in A - mer - i - ca!
ver - y big deal in A - mer - i - ca!

3

(Instrumental)

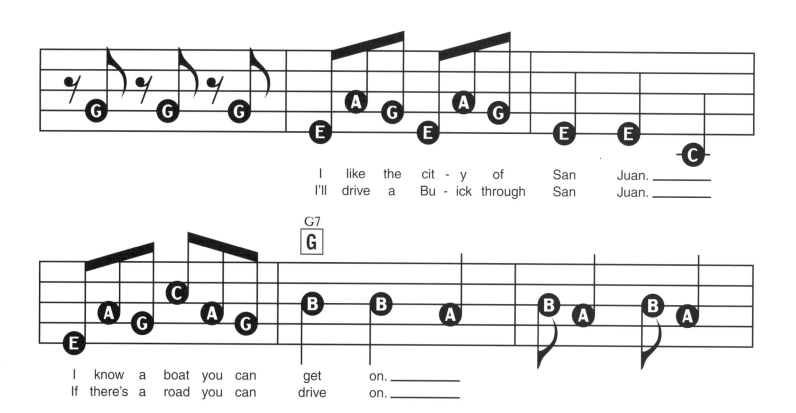

I like the cit - y of San Juan. _____
I'll drive a Bu - ick through San Juan. _____

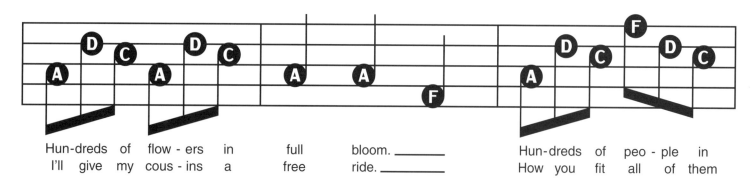

G7

I know a boat you can get on. _____
If there's a road you can drive on. _____

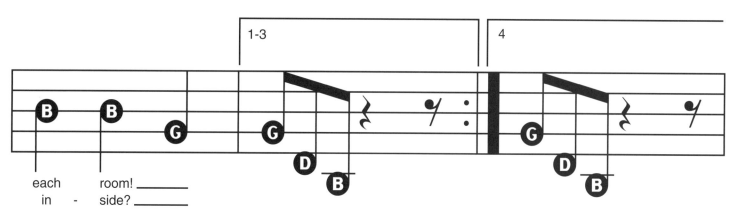

Hun-dreds of flow - ers in full bloom. _____
I'll give my cous - ins a full free ride. _____

Hun-dreds of peo - ple in
How you fit all of them

1-3

4

each room! _____
in - side? _____

4

Chorus

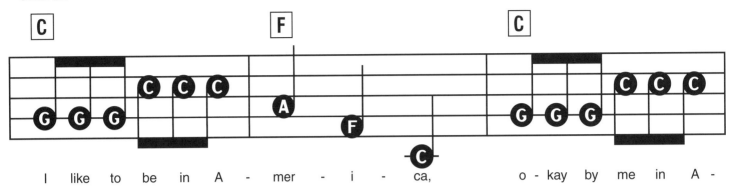

I like to be in A - mer - i - ca, o-kay by me in A -

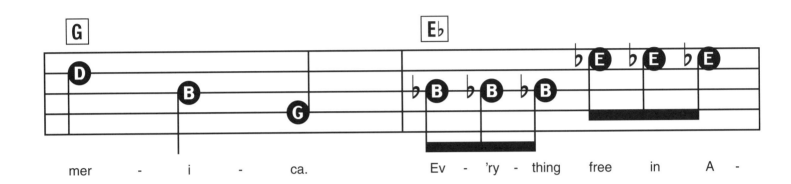

mer - i - ca. Ev - 'ry - thing free in A -

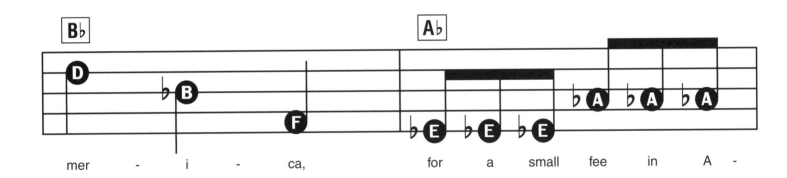

mer - i - ca, for a small fee in A -

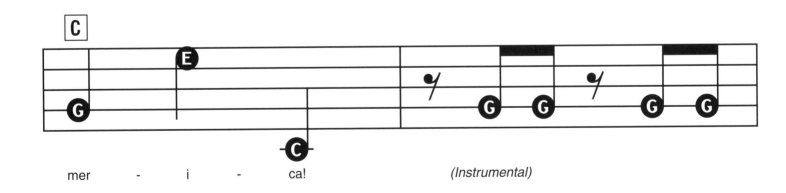

mer - i - ca! *(Instrumental)*

Additional Lyrics

3. Immigrant goes to America,
   Many hellos in America.
   Nobody knows in America,
   Puerto Rico's in America!
   When I will go back to San Juan.
   When you will shut up and get gone?
   I'll give them new washing machine.
   What have they got there to keep clean?
   Chorus

4. I like the shores of America,
   Comfort is yours in America.
   Knobs on the doors in America,
   Wall to wall floors in America!
   I'll bring a T.V. to San Juan.
   If there's a current to turn on.
   Ev'ryone there will give big cheer.
   Ev'ryone there will have moved here?
   Chorus

Cool

Registration 1
Rhythm: Jazz Pop or Swing

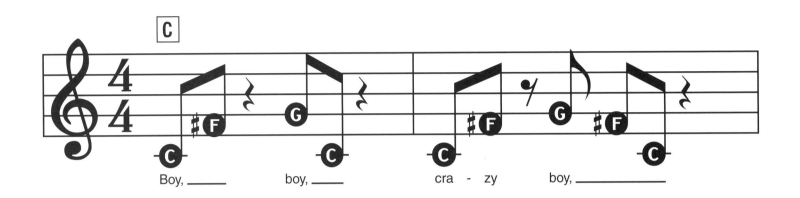

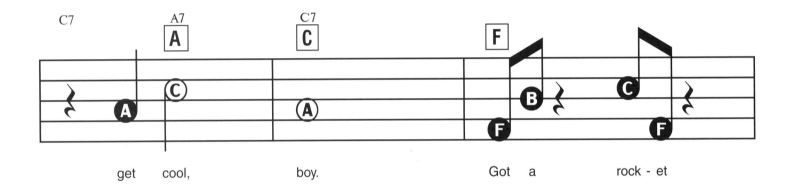

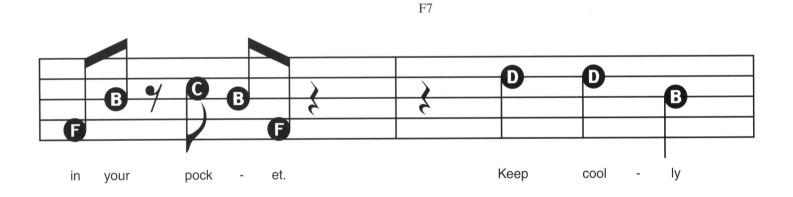

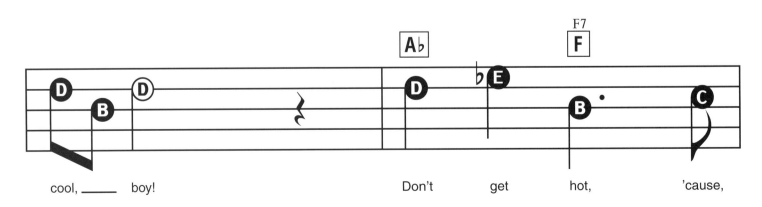

Lyrics by Stephen Sondheim
Music by Leonard Bernstein

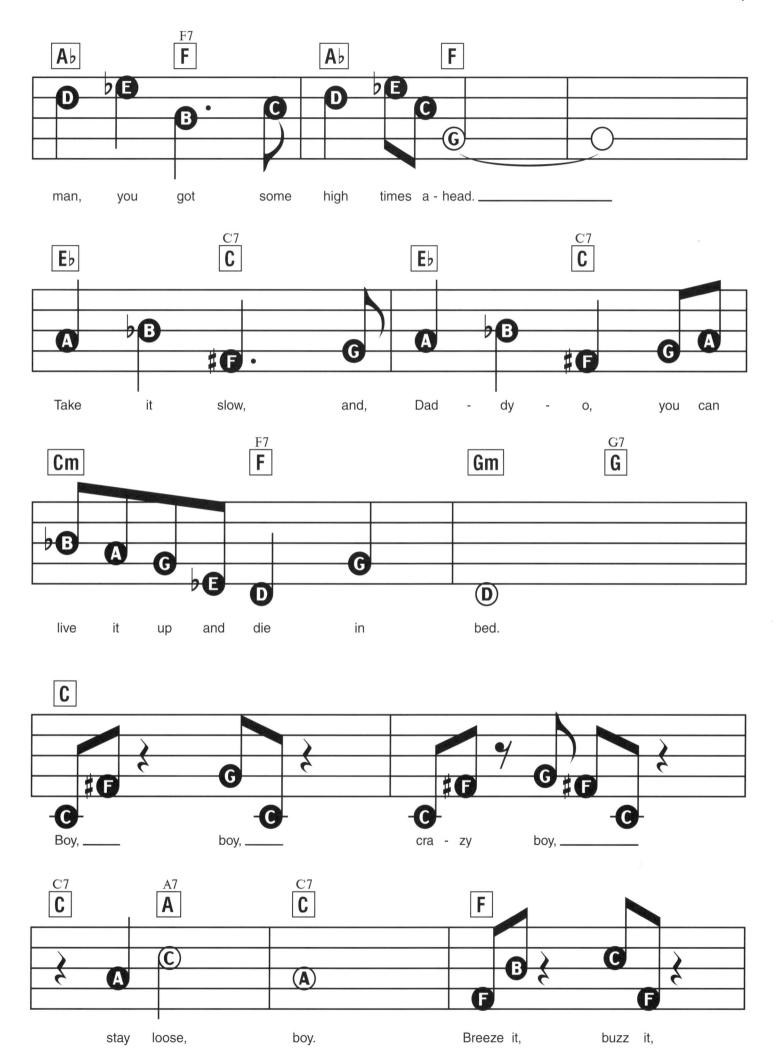

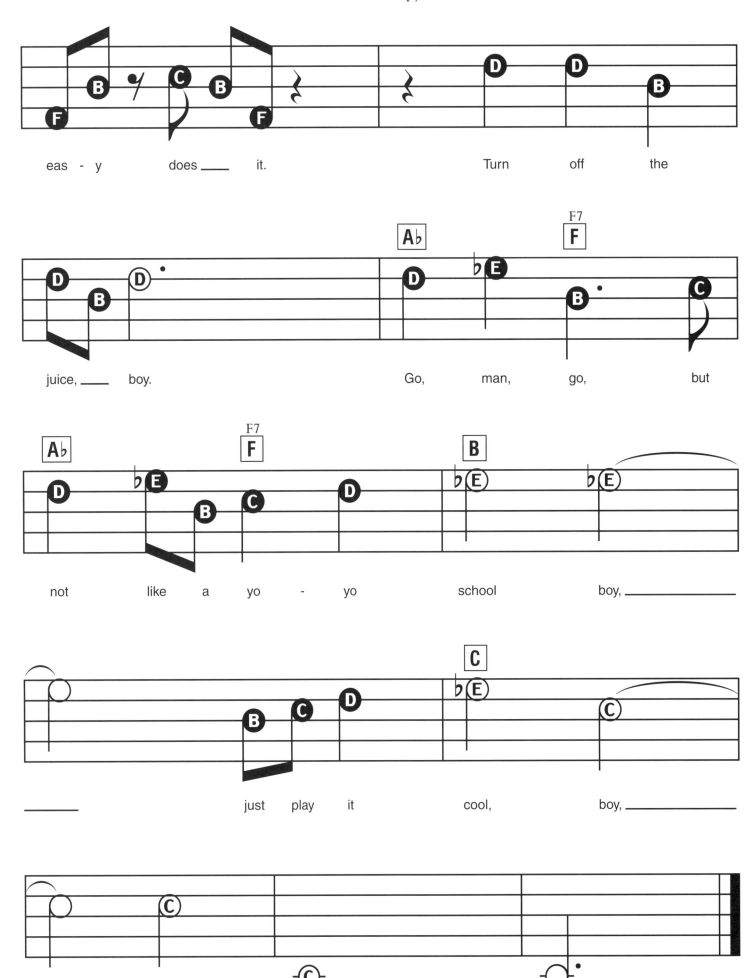

I Feel Pretty

Registration 8
Rhythm: Waltz

Lyrics by Stephen Sondheim
Music by Leonard Bernstein

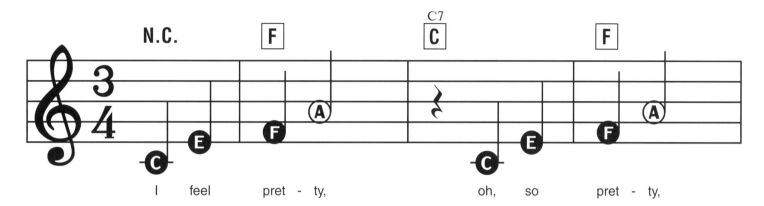

I feel pret - ty, oh, so pret - ty,

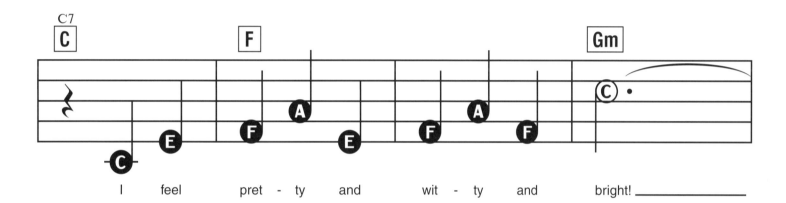

I feel pret - ty and wit - ty and bright! _____

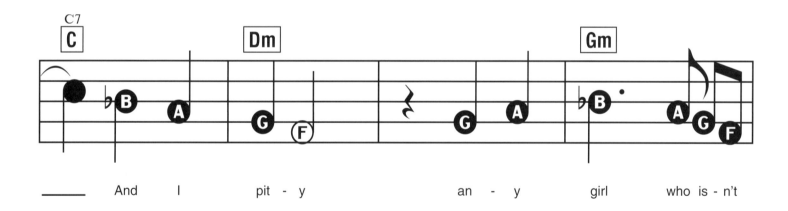

_____ And I pit - y an - y girl who is - n't

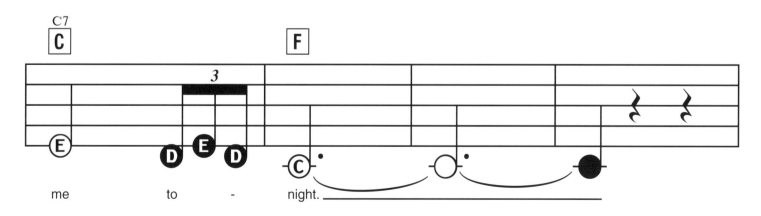

me to - night. _____

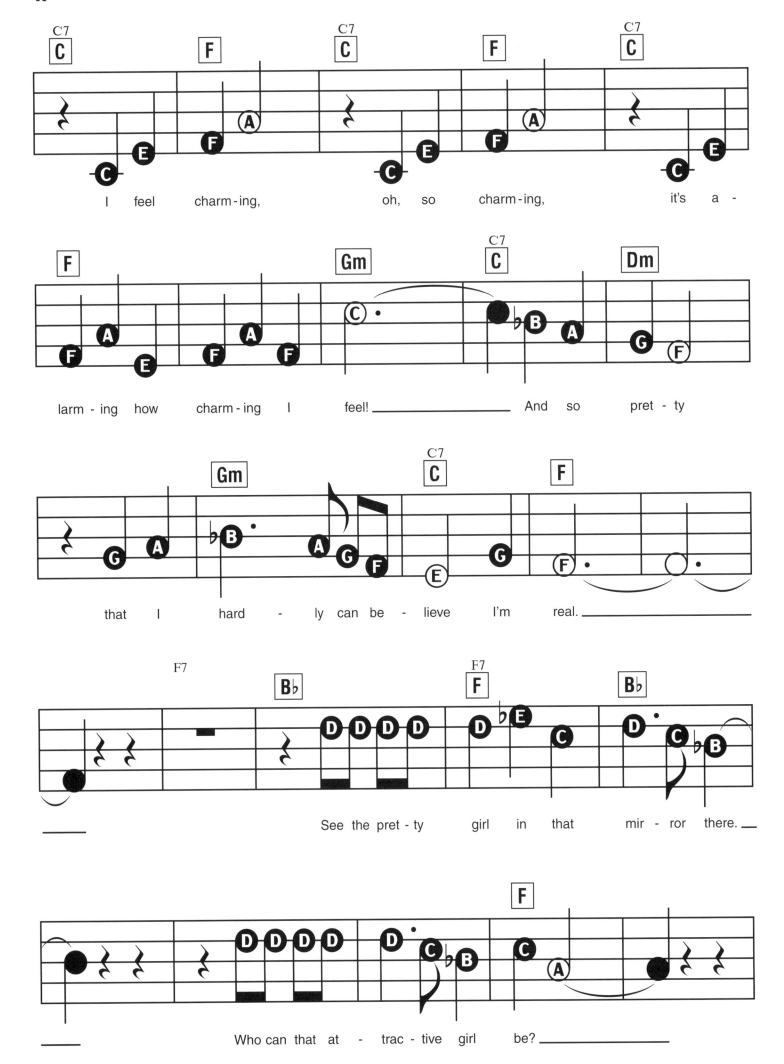

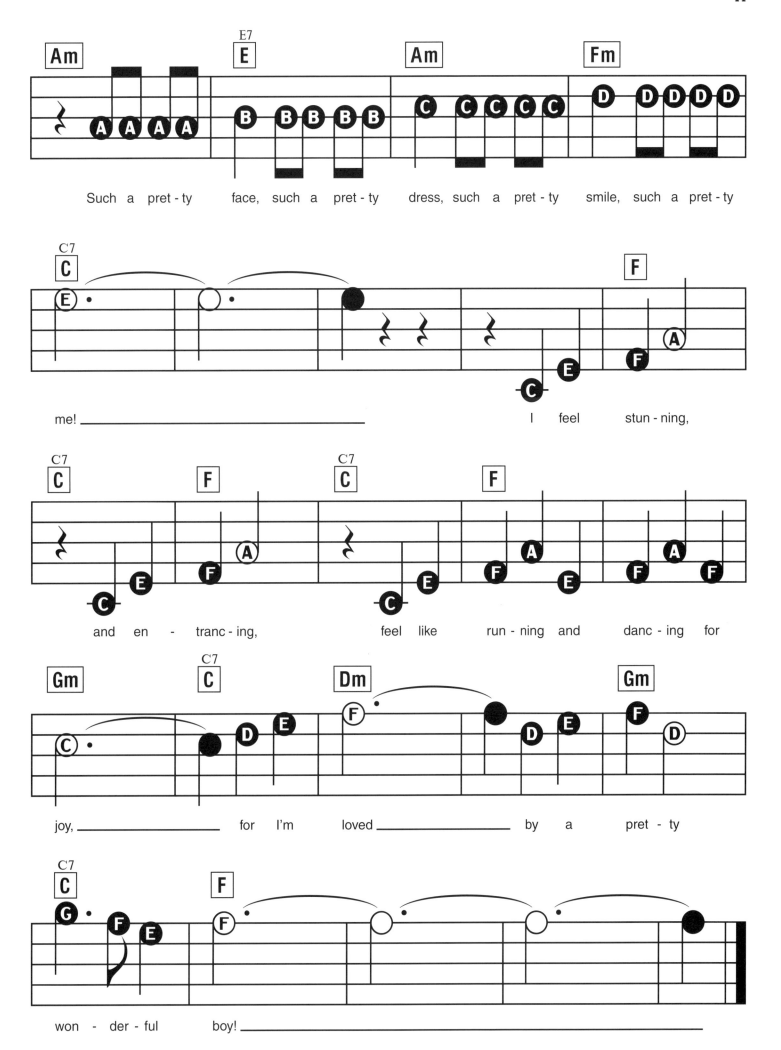

I Have a Love

Registration 3
Rhythm: 4/4 Ballad or 8 Beat

Lyrics by Stephen Sondheim
Music by Leonard Bernstein

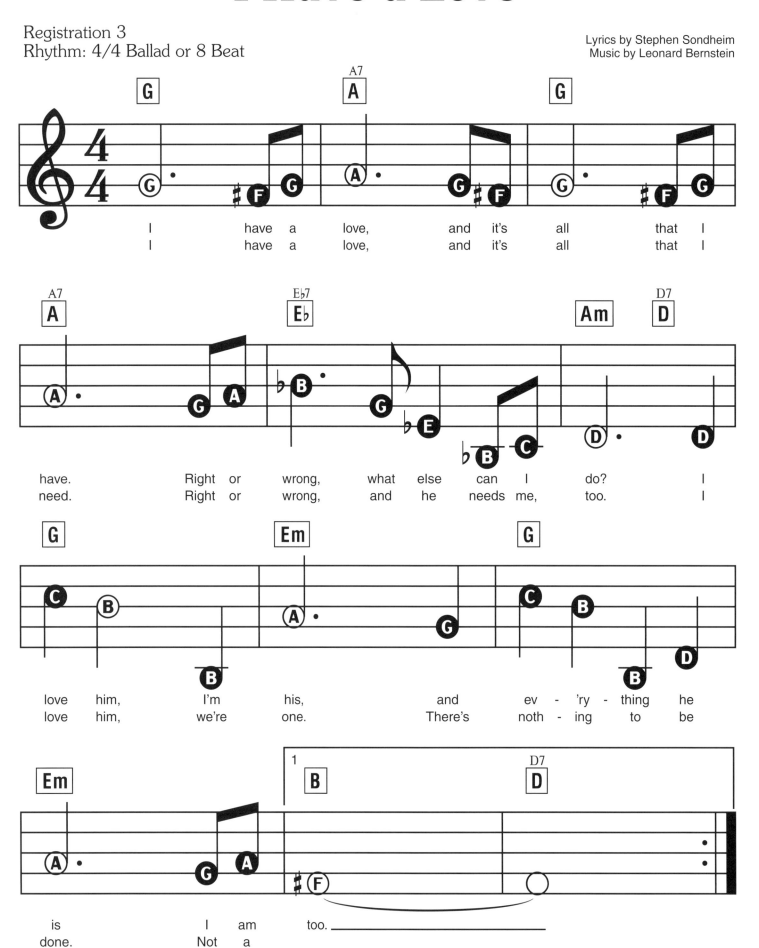

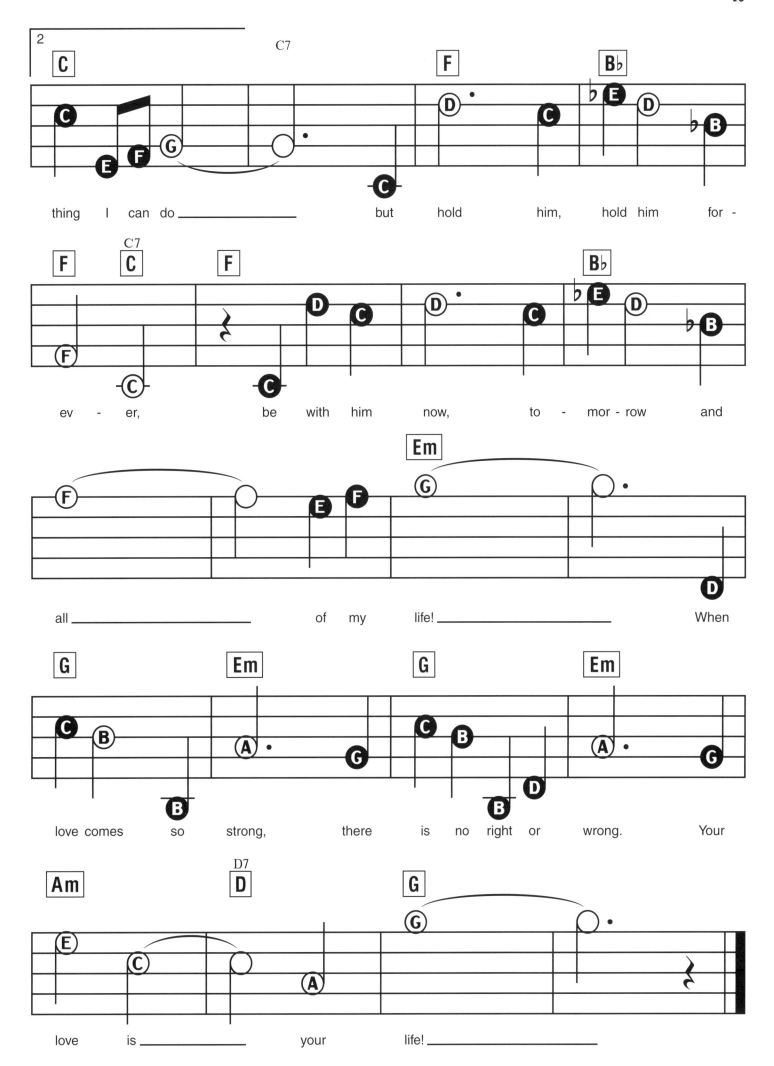

Maria

Registration 3
Rhythm: Bossa Nova, Latin, or Pops

Lyrics by Stephen Sondheim
Music by Leonard Bernstein

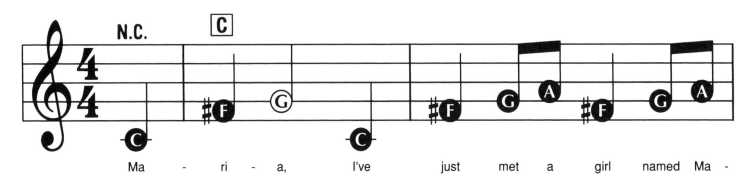

Ma - ri - a, I've just met a girl named Ma -

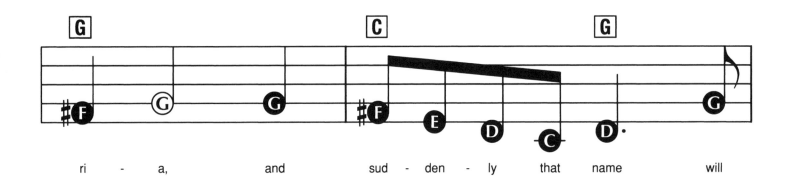

ri - a, and sud - den - ly that name will

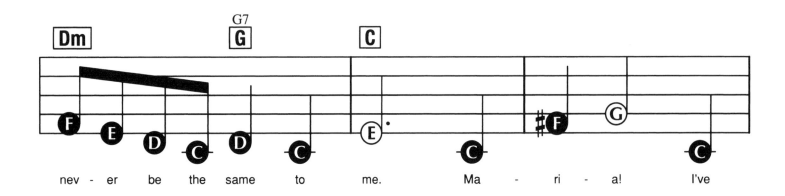

nev - er be the same to me. Ma - ri - a! I've

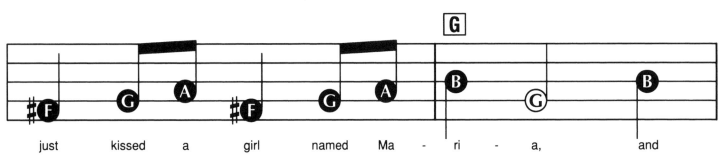

just kissed a girl named Ma - ri - a, and

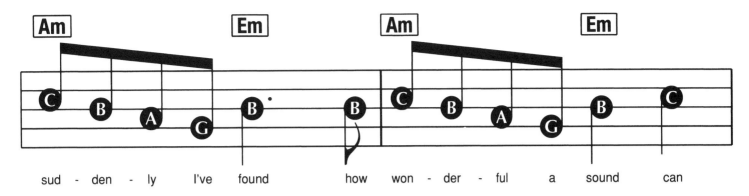

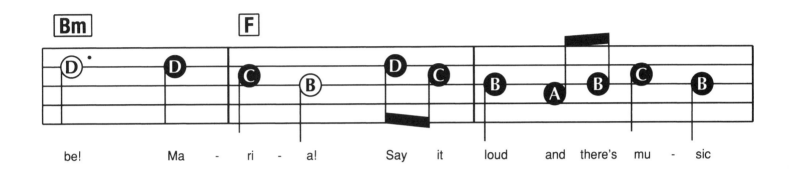

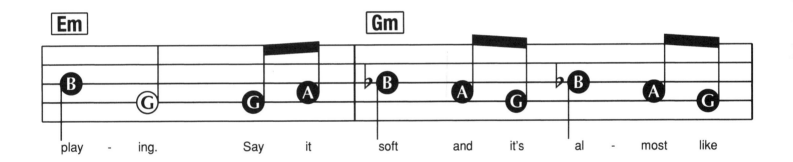

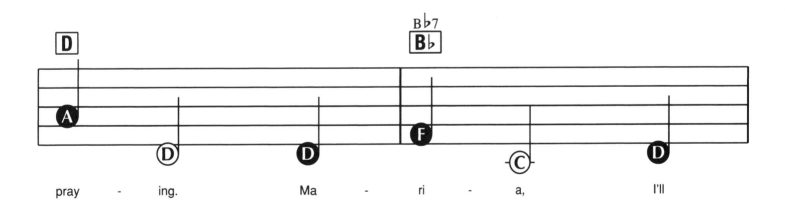

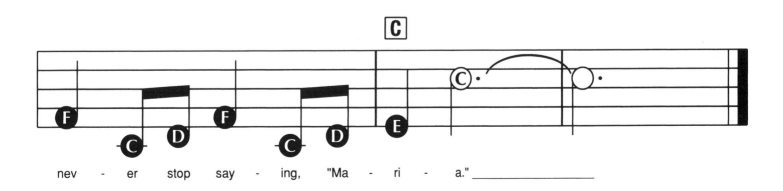

One Hand, One Heart

Registration 8
Rhythm: Waltz

Lyrics by Stephen Sondheim
Music by Leonard Bernstein

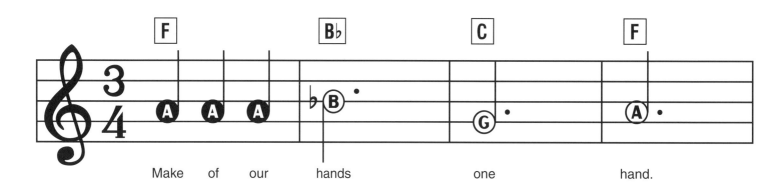

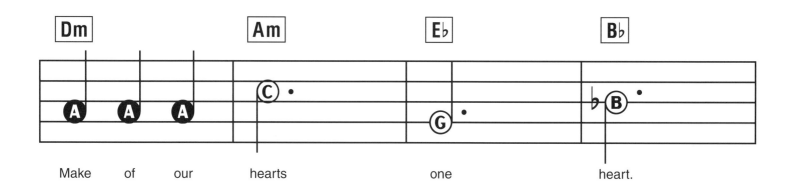

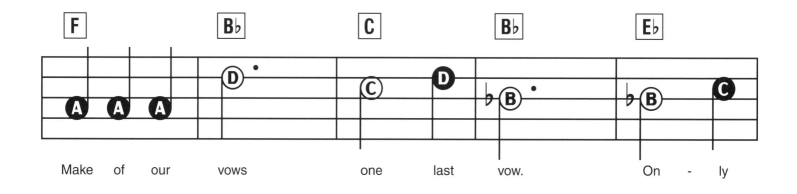

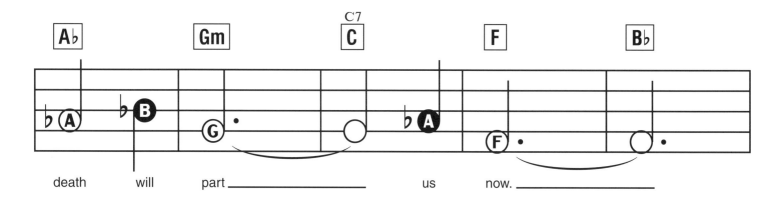

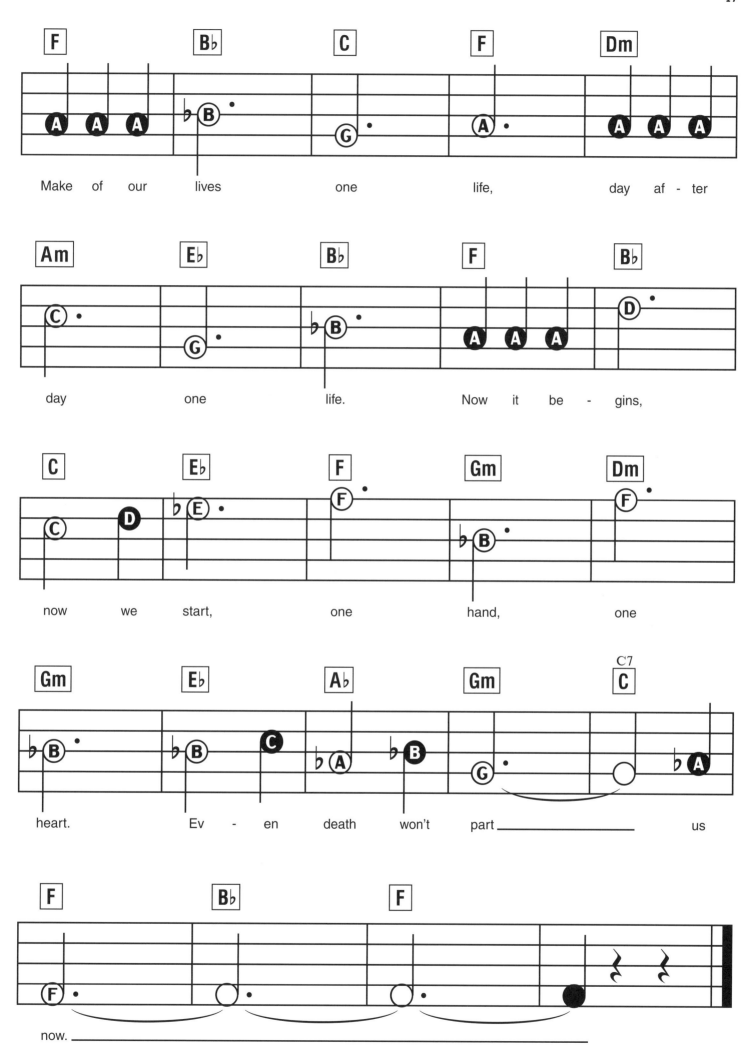

Promenade from the Dance at the Gym

Registration 2
Rhythm: March

Music by Leonard Bernstein

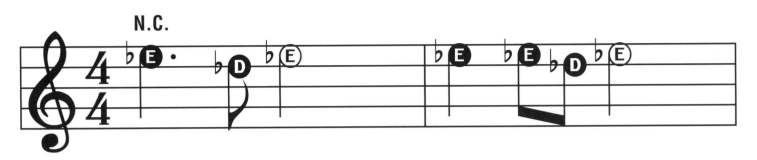

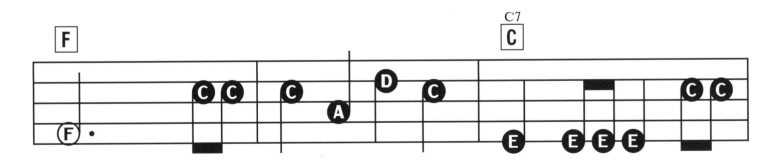

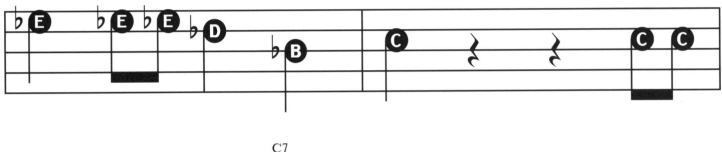

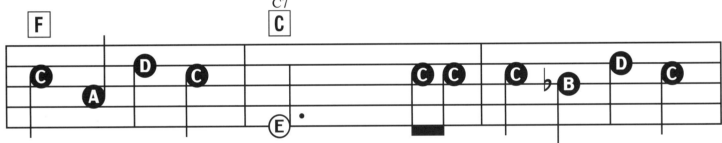

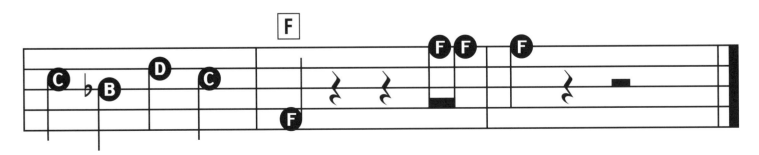

Somewhere

Registration 1
Rhythm: Slow Rock or Ballad

Lyrics by Stephen Sondheim
Music by Leonard Bernstein

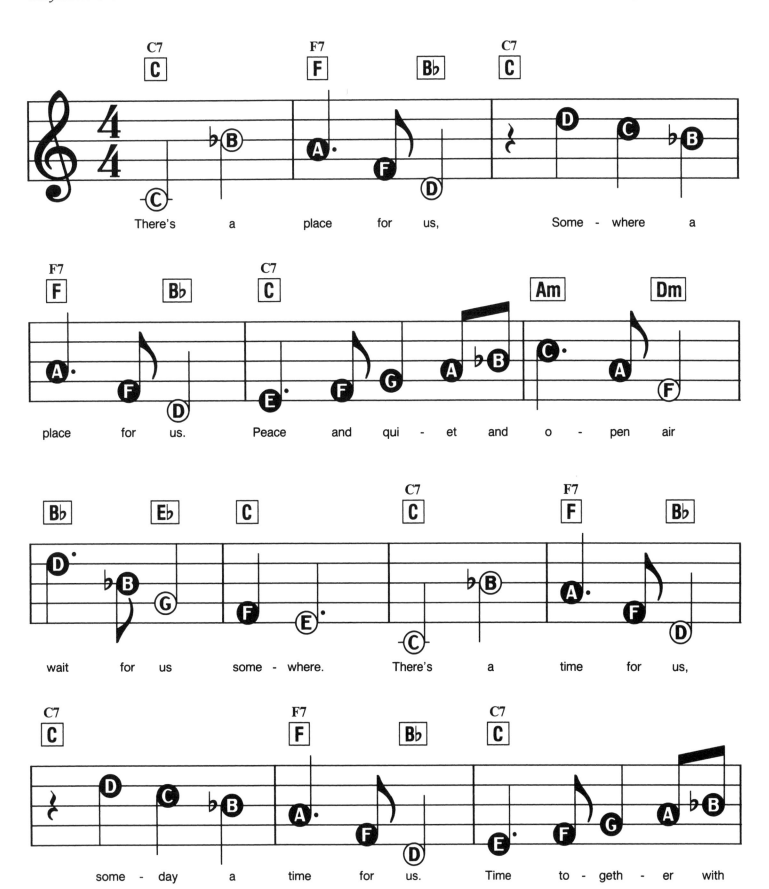

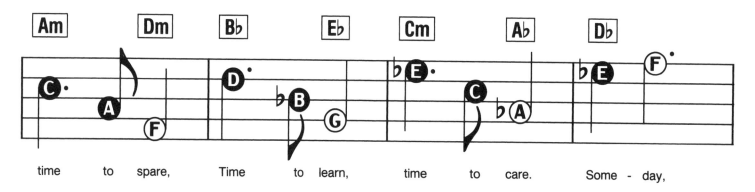

time to spare, Time to learn, time to care. Some - day,

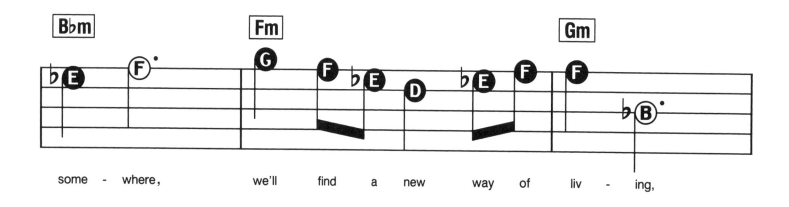

some - where, we'll find a new way of liv - ing,

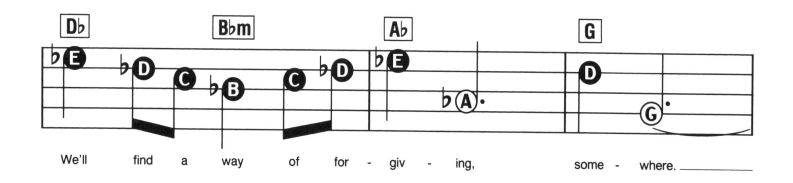

We'll find a way of for - giv - ing, some - where. _____

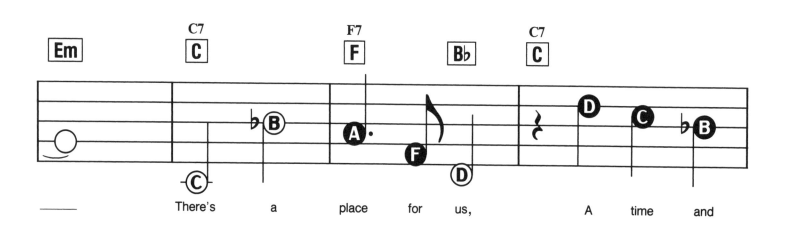

_____ There's a place for us, A time and

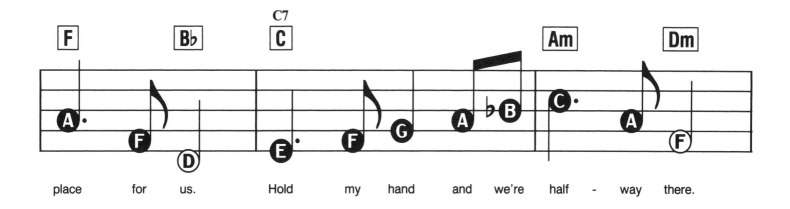

place for us. Hold my hand and we're half - way there.

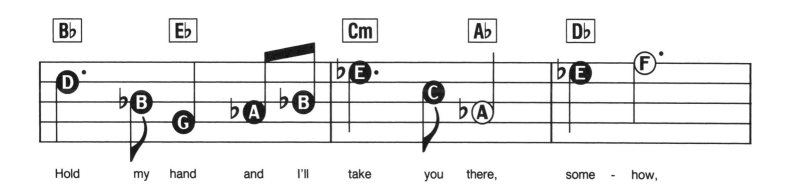

Hold my hand and I'll take you there, some - how,

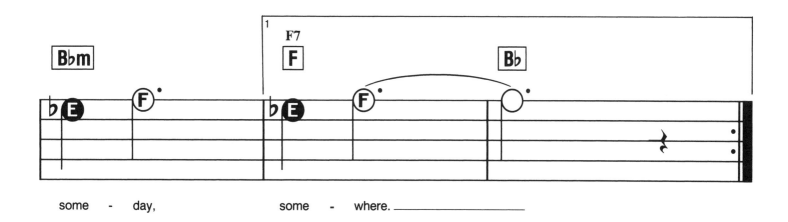

some - day, some - where. _____

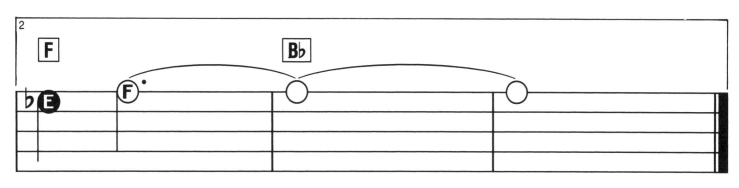

some - where. _____

Tonight

Registration 5
Rhythm: Beguine or Latin

Lyrics by Stephen Sondheim
Music by Leonard Bernstein

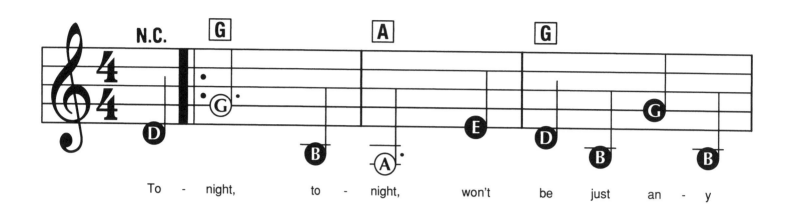

To - night, to - night, won't be just an - y

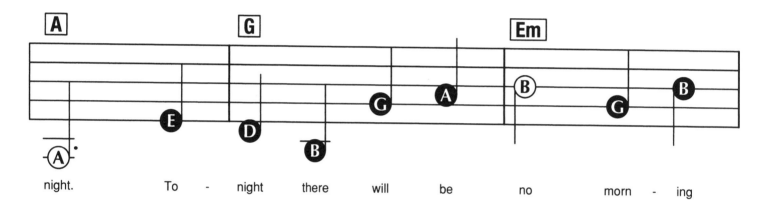

night. To - night there will be no morn - ing

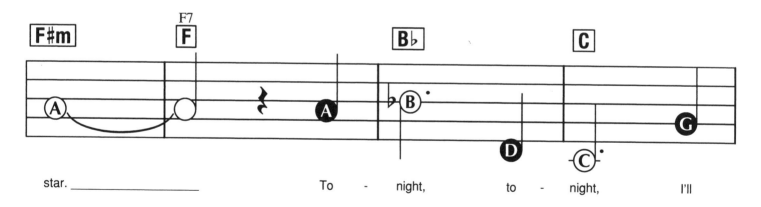

star. _____ To - night, to - night, I'll

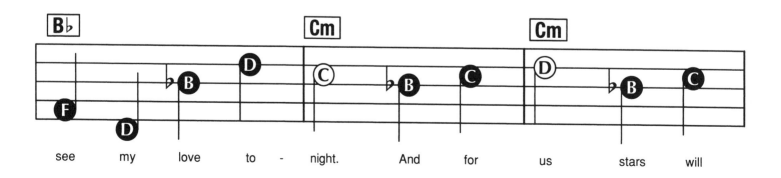

see my love to - night. And for us stars will

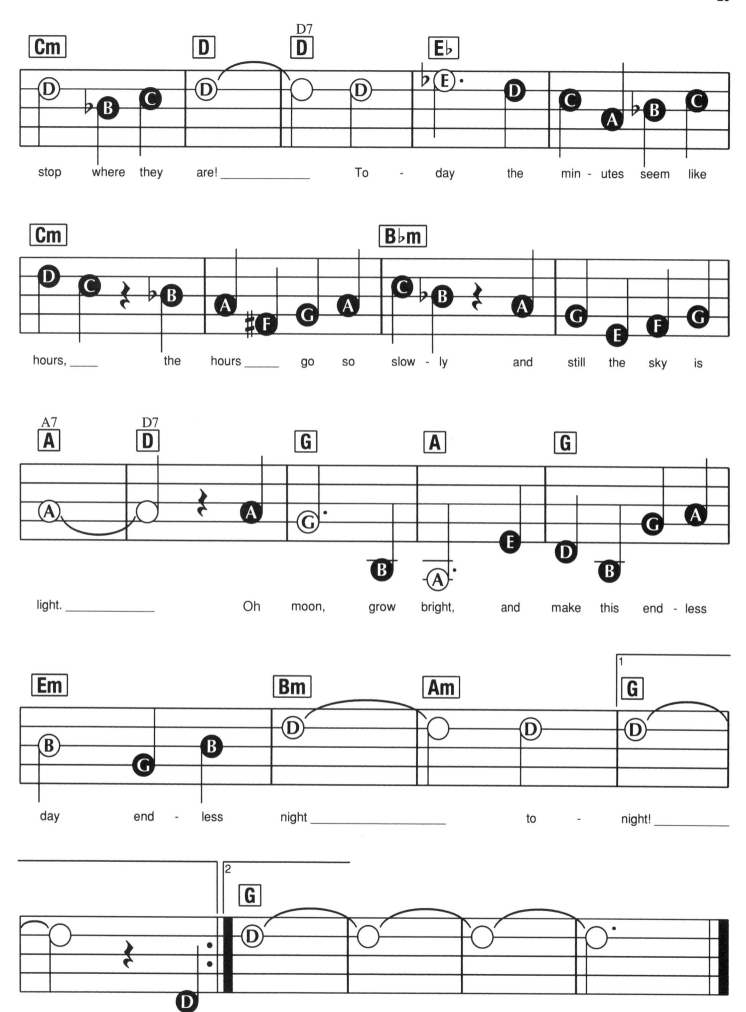